ONE BEAUTIFUL THING

CAROL DAVIS

Published in Australia by Sid Harta Books & Print Pty Ltd,

ABN: 34632585293

23 Stirling Crescent, Glen Waverley, Victoria 3150 Australia

Telephone: +61 3 9560 9920, Facsimile: +61 3 9545 1742

E-mail: author@sidharta.com.au

First published in Australia 2024

This edition published 2025

Copyright text and photographs © Carol Davis 2024

Cover design, typesetting: WorkingType (www.workingtype.com.au)

The right of Carol Davis to be identified as the
Author of the Work has been asserted in accordance with the
Copyright, Designs and Patents Act 1988.

This book is a work of fiction. Any similarities to that of
people living or dead are purely coincidental.

All rights reserved. No part of this publication may be reproduced, stored in a retrieval system, or transmitted, in any form or by any means without the prior written permission of the publisher, nor be otherwise circulated in any form of binding or cover other than that in which it is published and without a similar condition being imposed on the subsequent purchaser.

ISBN: 978-1-922958-83-9

About the Author

Carol Davis has lived and worked in Brisbane, Queensland, for most of her life.

She has written many books of poetry over the years and it remains her greatest passion.

Surprising herself, she has worked in the field of nursing for over forty years and continues to do so.

She is also a massage therapist and reiki master, a mediocre guitar player and not an altogether bad singer.

Her ambition is to see the poetry sections of bookstores become much bigger and more visible.

Introduction

I think it's pretty safe to say that my life did not turn out the way I planned. Maybe a better way to put it is that my life did not turn out the way I imagined or the way I dreamed.

As I can see more clearly now – from this distance, that part of the 'trouble' was that I haven't really been a planner. The words 'goal setting' were never part of my vocabulary.

I've pretty much just rocked along with the ebb and flow of life. I guess I've been a bit of a dreamer.

Although I've always kind of known what I didn't want and I had some ideas of what I wanted my life to look like, I can't say that I planned my future. A five-year plan – what is that?

I've had some difficulty in dealing with life and I've mostly blamed myself for that. Maybe I've been a bit too sensitive. I haven't always made wise decisions and I haven't been a great lover of my career. Sometimes, I was a depressive individual. Oh, I could go on and on.

And I've blamed others as well – oh yes, I have.

In fact, my default setting has been 'victim'. My inner me has found it quite easy, normal almost, to look at the negative in any, shall we say, challenging life event. Being positive was harder for me.

Now some people will find this a bit unbelievable because

I'm great at covering things up. I'm an expert at it. I should have been on the stage, as they say.

But others are nodding because they know. They know my struggle. They see me. Well, they understand me as much as anyone can understand another person and let's face it — that's only maybe fifty percent at best.

But much to my surprise and despite my lack of a sensible plan, I arrived at an age where I am now considered a senior. And just lately, I've come to accept the type of person I am. I accept the fact that I've done the best I could with the 'material' I had to work with.

Some dreams have come to fruition. And yes, there's been many failures. If I had my time over again — sure, I'd make some, maybe many, different choices. I have not always been the best version of myself. But I have sought to be. I have tried.

I don't think I am alone in this. Just the other day in fact, I read a quote that said, 'The only failure is in never trying.' Good one that.

And do you know what I've been thinking lately? I've been thinking that you can't lay that blame on yourself. Or anyone else. I've decided to give myself a break and let go of thinking that things should have been better. I should have been better. They should have been better.

You know what? I, we, they, were pretty okay.

Maybe it's just part of our karmic journey. Maybe it's written somewhere. Maybe God has other plans for us. Maybe it's just the way life goes.

But I think if you've tried not to hurt people, if you've tried to love some people and if you've tried to face life head on and do what you can, you've done pretty well. And maybe it's not so great compared to some. That's okay too.

In the end, none of the what-ifs and why nots and why didn't you(s) matter because you did what you could. You ran your race.

We really are unique. A one off with all our foibles and mistakes and stresses – our wins and our losses. We've made it to here by trying and being, after all, the best version of ourselves.

However, it's not always easy to see the bright side, the positive, the wisdom that life teaches us.

Sometimes, we falter…

So, what on earth has all this got to do with this book?

Well, one day, on my way into work, I was feeling quite a bit down in the mouth about everything, I saw a red leaf on green grass and I thought – how beautiful.

And I kept looking…

Maybe not every day.

But often from then on.

I kept looking.

For at least One … Beautiful …Thing.

I made it my mission.

My reason to keep smiling.

I realised that my default setting had, ever so slowly, begun to change. Instead of the 'glass half empty,' I found myself slowly changing to the 'glass half full' kind of person. It's a work in progress for me.

I think maybe, if we all tried looking for that One Beautiful Thing every day, we could change the way we look at our lives.

And if we are all out there doing that — I think we could change our world, the planet, the universe. I think it could be a global phenomenon!

Give it a go.

See what you think.

So here is some of my poetry on this theme, more or less. I've written it over a lifetime and when I look back and read some of the older ones, I realise that I have had some pretty beautiful moments. I've not always been 'the glass half empty' person. Perhaps, we are not who we think we are after all.

Carol

January 2024

This is for all of the dreamers. The poets.
The music makers. The free spirits. The wanderers.
The crazy ones. The sad ones. The ones who lost hope. The ones who found hope. The highflyers and the ones who just wanted to fly away.
And for the ones who made plans. And for the others who didn't.

And this is for my family. I got lucky with you.

Contents

About The Author	Iii
Introduction	V
Contents	X
One Beautiful Thing	1
Never Judge a Book By its Cover	4
In A Hurry	6
Trousers	7
Budgie	8
Breaking Down The Barriers	9
Beginnings	10
Homeless	11
Winter	14
Hanging In, Not Up	15
Miracle	16
Mum and Dad	18
The Inspector	20
Looking	22
Creator	25
Storm: Part 1	30
Storm: Part 2	31

Asking	33
Flitty, Bitty	34
Slitherings	35
Clouds	38
Hours And Hours	39
Oops	42
Beauty Lies in the Eye of the Beholder?	44
Peace	46
For Nanna	48
On A Midnight Train	50
Stargazer	52
Just Sitting	53
The Orthopaedic Outpatients' Department	56
Life Is A River	64
Letting Go	69
Human	72
Celebrating	75
This Is	76
A Trail in the Woods	78
Rattled	80

Music	83
Till the Night is Done	85
A Gift of Love	87
Spring Flowers	88
Simple Pleasures	92
Lucky	94
That's How I Knew	95
What Colour is Love?	97
Sometimes	99
Music	101
A Song is a Good Conversation	102
Home	107
Nature	111
Fly	112
Escape	113
I Need…	114
Gone	116
Soul	117
Forest	118
Bring Me Here	119

Letting Go	122
Better	124
Wouldn't I?	125
Calling to Me	126
Summer and Winter	128
For Chris	129
You and I	131
We are One	134
The Time of Your Life	136
Requiem	138
Light	140
Identity	142
One Little Boat	145
Will I?	148
Never Forget	151
Finding Home	154
If	155
Still Looking	156

ONE BEAUTIFUL THING

Open your eyes

Forget the pain

Or maybe because of it

Starting your day

Defeated before beginning,

Decide not to be

It's not what you want

It's not where you want to be

How to keep going

Tired out

With wanting something

Anything

This is not how it is meant to be

Why me

Why not

What lead to this moment

What leads me away

Open your eyes

When nothing can change

Try seeing with new eyes

Look for it

It may be so small

And inconsequential

But

It will be there

Keep looking

There will be…

One beautiful thing

Write it down

That's the one for today

And there might be another

Next day

Every day

Keep looking

Write it down

It's a discipline

Like exercise

Every day

Search for

One beautiful thing

It can become

Many beautiful things

Your focus changes

Transformation begins

Not what you dreamed of

But what you have

Not what might have been

But what is

And suddenly

One day

You wake up

In not as much pain

And you realise

Your world

Is infinitely better

Infinitely

Beautiful

NEVER JUDGE A BOOK BY ITS COVER

Oh, he was a big smelly guy sitting right next to me

on a crowded smelly bus

full of disconnected commuters

wanting to get home

solemn faces and no one looking or speaking to anyone else

The traffic was so bad

just one mechanical jerk after another

I thought I might just suffocate

wedged in by his massiveness

breathing in his stale odour

He talked to the young man across from him

Yes, actually engaged in conversation

and in response to something

he let out the most amazing high-pitched giggle

It was so surprising

so funny

they kept talking

he kept giggling

blow me down, but you couldn't help smiling

and I noticed that there were other smiles

He was infectious

In the most beautiful way

IN A HURRY

It was obvious that she was in a hurry.
But she came back to hold her little girl's hand one more time through the fence of the childcare centre.
The look of loving delight on that child's face was so beautiful.
If you could, you would bottle that.

TROUSERS

Both in a hurry, harried, waiting to be served.

Knowing there was such a short window of opportunity.

Distracted I looked at her trousers

Oh, I love your pants

I didn't mean to say it out loud.

She was surprised, pleased and we had a conversation about trousers.

We got served

And both left with smiles.

BUDGIE

There are bad, sad days.
And that's okay.
My budgie can still make me smile
with her ridiculous behaviour.

BREAKING DOWN THE BARRIERS

In this unfamiliar corporate world
I wonder what the hell I am doing here
Where I so obviously don't belong
Pushed into a busy noisy city working life
So far from where I think I'd like to be
And the automatons surround me with their
smart suits and earphones and walking-talking jargon.
Words I don't understand.
Feelings I don't begin to share.

Then one by one, they need me.
I have something of my own that I can give
To help them through.
And suddenly I find a shared language.

Understanding our similar stories and emotions.
Breaking down the barriers
Underneath their corporate coats of protection.
I am humbled to discover
Real people.
And I have found a place to be.

BEGINNINGS

I much prefer the lateness of a sunset
but I have to get up with the sun.
Sigh … one beautiful sunrise after another.

HOMELESS

I see you

sad person,

looking down

away from the flow

of others

around you.

Your cap of coins,

your thin dirty blanket,

your bag —

these are your world.

Surrounded by the cold,

hard, street pavements,

you sit, you lie,

you sleep.

How did you get to be here,

sad person?

What is your story about?

What went wrong?

My heart cries out

for you.

Have you no choices,

no people,

no tribe?

I'm fearful

that I could be you.

I don't know what to do

to help you.

Do you think that I

don't want to?

You would be wrong

and I think of you

often.

You have become

a part of my day.

HOMELESS

I reach down to give you

some part of myself

this poem

and a twenty.

Not near enough.

I walk past

like all the others

but

sad person

I see you.

WINTER

Don't go too soon

Winter sun

I love your bright warmth

Coming through my window

Falling in welcome rays across

My chair.

It calls me to come sit

Be still

Enjoy the winter day.

Cosy and content.

Summer comes all too soon

With its boisterous sun

And lively heat

We look for breezes

Longing for cool

But always busy, busy

Racing through our days

Summer is vibrancy.
Winter is a comfy chair on a cosy afternoon.

HANGING IN, NOT UP

One difficult customer's phone call

Not what she wanted to hear

But she listened

And that's all it took

To make peace.

MIRACLE

I've done all I can.

I've tried every single way that I can think of.

I'll keep trying.

But I'm giving it up to you.

Putting it out there.

Asking for help.

Waiting.

Hoping.

For your miracle.

And then you answered.

Courage.

Persistence.

Belief.

MUM AND DAD

I've loved writing all my life. I loved that slate in first grade. I loved doing copy book writing. I loved when we had to do compositions and essays. I've loved making up stories and writing poetry and prose. I've loved it and I've needed to do it. It's like oxygen to me. I can't do without writing.

It took me a long while though, to call myself a writer and a poet. I don't think I ever felt worthy of those titles. I didn't feel good enough. Now there's an oft repeated refrain. Familiar?

I've written a few books of poetry and the last one I wrote was a rather sad one. I had looked after my parents for a long while and eventually, they died. It was a compilation of my writing over that period of time. There was a lot of grief in there. It can still make me cry. But in the end, it was about hope and renewal. It was about being lucky and remembering how beautiful it was to have known them. How beautiful they were.

I had your beautiful smile every day for fifty-seven years.
I'll remember it for the rest of this life
And the ones to come.

I had your strength for sixty-one years of my life.
I'll take it with me for whatever remains.
Into the light.

I will smile for you
And try to be strong.
And remember the beautiful days with both of you.

THE INSPECTOR

A raven

The only one still on duty

Up and down the scaffolding

Looking into pipe hollows

Inspecting and interested

Ignoring the traffic parade

Busy, busy

Checking stuff

One hollow catches his attention

He sticks his entire head inside

Something wrong?

Something right

A nice juicy morsel of something

Hidden away

Thinking it was safe

A late afternoon treat

For the construction raven

Doing his rounds.

*

My bus was stuck in Friday traffic

Near the new high-rise being built

And I looked through the window at him

But the raven didn't see me.

LOOKING

I am humbled

By the minutiae

Of Nature

Seeking nothing

Not even to be looked at

Just being

Going about its business

Behind the scenes.

I had been looking upwards

Into the dreaming of clouds

I had been looking outwards

Waiting and hoping for…

But one day

I looked down

And was enraptured to find

The simplest of amazing things

One red leaf on a sea of green

And suddenly my world

Took on an explosion

Of a million small

Miracle moments

As Nature revealed

All of her secrets

To my opening eyes

To my opening mind

And to my laughing surprise.

Sometimes in our quest

For the big picture

We fail to see

All the tiny images

That make up

ONE BEAUTIFUL THING

One beautiful drop

In an ocean

Of our day

Our life

Our being

On my busy morning journey

All it took for happiness

Was a single red leaf

On a sea of green.

CREATOR

I am the creator of all things worthwhile.
I am the bridge between you and me.
Between the old and the new.
Between what is past and what is now.
Between all understanding and letting go.

I am the creator of pure air,
flowing through my lungs, my whole body.
Lifting me up on a beautiful breeze.
Higher and higher.
Above all things.
Drifting into stars and laughter.

I am the creator of the clear, clean, natural water
that floats my body and my boat.
That lifts me through the weightless, effortless swim
of my dreams.

I am the creator of the fire wherein
I cast my doubts
my disbeliefs
my limiting self-image
and my opinions.
My pessimism.
My protective devices.
My misjudgements.
And all the ropes that bind.
All the things I need no more.
And never did.
Creating a bonfire so beautiful and so bright
that you will see it from where you are.
And I will rejoice in it
from where I am.

I am the creator of all my wishes,
prayers, dreams and aspirations.
I am the creator of them,
simple and true; to serve me well.
In my life and after life.

I am the creator of all my experiences.
Every.
Single.
One.
I am the teacher and the student
of all the necessary lessons that bought me here.

I am the creator of all love.
My heart is open and never-endingly full.
Because that is what I want.
That is why I am here.
For my life and after life.
And for all life.

I am the creator of my peace of mind, body, soul and spirit.
I am the light that does not diminish.

I am the creator of all things worthwhile.
Even the things I didn't know were worthwhile.
I am the bridge between you and me.
Between my soul and my salvation.
Between all my understanding and my letting go.

I am.

Only me.

Only me.

Only me.

Now.

STORM

Part 1

There's a storm out on the ocean
black to the horizon and
quietly menacing.

Run little boat, run for the harbour.
No need to test the wrath
of mighty Nature.
She will surely win.

There's a storm out on the ocean.
Darkly it comes.
No place for a little boat
who plays in the sun.

Stealthily, it is coming
amazing, entrancing.
Run little boat, run.

STORM

Part 2

Four bells clang over a grey sea.

Waves whipped up.

Crashing on rocks.

  There is a storm coming.

Four bells clang under a darkening sky.

And sea-birds are on the wing.

  There is a storm coming.

One bell for the north and one for the south.

A ring for the east.

A clang for the west.

Wishing all souls upon the sea a safe harbour.

Time to hunker down.

  There is a storm coming.

As they always do and always will.

Listen for the bells.

Heed the warning signs.

Feel it in your heart and all will be well.

One is for the north to where you are heading.

One is for the south from where you have been.

One is for the east and the light that is coming.

And one for the west that is home.

Four bells ringing

let this be your beacon.

  There is a storm coming.

  A beautiful one.

ASKING

I miss you like falling rain.
Send me your voices to ease my pain.
Send me your voices to sustain.
Till I am with you all again.

Send me your help, your hope, your love.
From deep below or far above.
And I, I will in turn be
the strength
the hope
the help.
The love.

FLITTY, BITTY

Why do you, Willy, wag your tail?

In your busy, flitty, wag-tail way.

Do you, Willy, have a story to tell?

Or do you bring a message?

Or do you, Willy, simply like

to wag your flitty, bitty,

little black tail?

SLITHERINGS

Treading softly,
slowly.
Down to the green dream of
grassy summer softness.

Tiptoeing
and whispers only.
Do they have ears?
Surprise is the key.

In a flash
they run away in
every direction.
But we were so quiet.

Why their panic
I wonder
Living as we do
together.

Long sleek
Beautiful, bronze beasts.
Heads up, tails down.
Where from, where to?

Under rocks,
heading for bushes,
leaves and long grass.
Back to invisible shelters.

Down in our backyard,
our own prehistoric,
reptile park.
Browns in the greens.

Going about their business,
quietly,
sneakily,
warily,
nervously.

They see you
before you see them,
leaving behind their
slitherings!

CLOUDS

I have re-discovered, quite late in life, a passion for clouds. I can't stop looking at them. I love them all. I seem to remember long summer days in my childhood, when I would lie on my back on the grass and look up at the clouds and imagine all kinds of countries and castles in them. But then I got busy.

But now I look up and out all the time. I take innumerable photos of them and post them on social media. I'm sure people must be quite sick of my clouds by now.

I even have a book about clouds.

It's not such a bad thing, is it? To keep looking up?

HOURS AND HOURS

Hours, I have spent

Looking out my window

At the trees

And the wind in the leaves

And the clouds

And beyond them all

At the space between

Just staring into

Its nothingness.

Hours have gone by

In quiet contemplation

Of nothing much at all

And sometimes, thoughts of everything

Some would say that

I'm wasting my time

and it is true

I have many things that need to be done.

Yet, I sit and stare

And feel richer, rested

And more peaceful

for the hours

that I have spent

Looking out my window.

OOPS

Oops

Look up.

They've joined hands

all together.

Become quite large

all across the sky.

Darkened the day,

decided to stay

after all.

Hello

my cumulonimbus companions.

Are you going to rain?

BEAUTY LIES IN THE EYE OF THE BEHOLDER?

My toes are going crooked
I see with some surprise.
They used to be so nice and straight.
A little plump and small in size.

My skin is going all spotty.
Worrying freckles and crusty bits.
It used to be so pale and creamy-firm.
Now it doesn't seem to fit.

Like other pieces of the puzzle
that is my body now.
Sagging, gathering, widening.
And lots of aches somehow.

Growing older is an adventure.
Or so the optimists say.
But my body, ever changing,
has seen a better day.

I am swapping my pride for acceptance.
I am counting my days instead of years.
I am laughing at my ridiculousness.
And sometimes shedding tears.

For beautiful, young bodies
that time outgrows.
Surprising us, all of a sudden,
with spotty skin and crooked toes.

PEACE

Peace.

Where your head
and your heart
and your soul
are all in the one
place
at the same
time.

Peace.

When the past
and the future
yesterday
today
and tomorrow
are all just
now.

Peace.

When your whole
being
just has
one
gigantic
sigh.

Breathe.

Breath.

Peace.

FOR NANNA

Flowers for the love you bring.

Tears are for the joy.

Smiles for all the happy days with you in.

I have sailed a voyage that I call my life.

You have been a kind and gentle wind for me bringing me home.

Flowers are because I love you.

Tears because I care.

Smiles are for the days of my life
with you in them.

FOR NANNA

ON A MIDNIGHT TRAIN

I met a traveller
on a midnight train
who waxed lyrical
about the waning moon.

Who said that life was too
damned short
not to have a laugh
every day.

He had ten kids and was
only thirty-one.
He worked like
a navvy,
drank like a fish
and swore like a trooper.
But surprisingly and unexpectedly;
he had the heart
of a poet.

You can never tell

Just by looking

Can you?

STARGAZER

I wonder what is going on

on that star so brightly burning.

I wonder if there is…

a life to find up there.

And if there is,

do you think

that it might wonder…

wonder what on earth

is going on down here.

JUST SITTING

I'm sitting all alone.
The day is late
and things are very quiet.
I'm just enjoying thinking
free and clear.
Just sitting peacefully here.

I've been wondering about some things.
Looking at my life
and all the people
that I love so much.
And I've been wishing
that this time would stay
just this way.
So nice to be in.

Yes, I'm scared
of broken dreams, shattered schemes
losing this peace inside of me.
But sitting here, all alone
it doesn't really seem to matter.
I have you now, life.
Tomorrow may take it
but I have you now.
You give me hope and joy.
and I'm trying to give you
something in return.

I'm sitting all alone.
The day is late.
And things are very quiet.
I'm kind of peaceful
and I love some people and
I'm wondering if it could all
just stay this way
so nice to be in.

I wrote this poem forty-four years ago. A moment of such utter peace that astonishes me now.

Of course, nothing ever stays the same. There have been many challenges, tears and pain. Broken dreams and shattered schemes.

But I have been fortunate enough to have had many moments like these.

Beautiful moments.

THE ORTHOPAEDIC OUTPATIENTS' DEPARTMENT

All you have to do
if you forget your way
is follow the line
of broken people.

Hobbling, limping
wheeled or wobbling
plastered, braced or
put together somehow
some way.
And together we wended our way
into the orthopaedic
outpatients' department.

This is where you learn
about patience,
through queues and waiting
and being shuffled
back and forth.

THE ORTHOPAEDIC OUTPATIENTS' DEPARTMENT

It matters not
what time your
appointment card says.
You will be seen in the fullness
of the public health system's
time.

Hopefully, you'll get home
for tea.
Always helps though
to bring a packed lunch,
a drink,
a good, thick book
or knitting.

The really interesting thing though,
is that, when you are practicing
this patience;
you can listen, look and learn
about those other patients.

People's stories,

small tragedies,

larger dramas,

ongoing hardships,

acts of heroism,

vandalism,

foolishness

being

living

holding on.

In such close proximity

with nerves stretched taut,

it helps to make a friend.

Swap histories,

talk of families,

laugh a little.

It passes the time

and shares the feelings.

It helps to make a connection.

Some aren't happy.

Things not progressing so well.

Bones misbehaving.

Some natter and

some nod off.

Makes me think of what it must

have been like

in a bomb shelter

in the war

but now

waiting for different bombshells

to fall.

There's TV now
in amidst the
clutter of crutches.
But you need good eyesight
or not, if it's only
the soapies.

I wonder where
they're all going and
what happened and
where they came from.
The old, the young,
the lame, the sad,
the cheerful,
the frustrated.

All hoping to be fixed,

healed

and put back together again

like Humpty.

Sent on their way,

never to return

they hope.

We hope.

Alleluia

your name is called.

More waiting, but at least

closer to the light

at the end of the tunnel.

All your faith is
centred on these
fallible human beings
who may or may not
have the knowledge
and the expertise
to make you
whole again.

How lucky we are
that sometimes,
they get it right.
At least, they try.
We have someone
in which to put
our faith.
It's the best we have.

If you lose your way,
just follow the long line
of broken people.
and, ever so slowly,
humbly,
hopefully,
you will wend
your way
back home.

LIFE IS A RIVER

Life, I think, is like a river.
Sometimes a short river.
Sometimes quite a long one.
We are the flotsam and jetsam that travel down it
towards the sea.

The way is not always easy.
Sometimes it is
and quite fun and frivolous.
But...
Sometimes the way is hard
with strong, dark currents
that pull us down.

Rocks and sand banks mark the journey.
Just when you think it is all flowing along well;
BUMP!
you hit a rock and have to take some notice
of that.

A lot of the time
the rock feels too big
to get around or over.
You cling on for fear of being dumped
into the unknown.

Or maybe you get stuck on a sandbank
for…ages, it seems.
Stuck in a rut.
Going nowhere.
Feeling nothing.

But you get started again.
You learn about the vagaries of the river.
You learn how to know its depths;
master its eddies.
You become a little wiser
learn to avoid
some of the rocks.
Learn to look out for other ones

and embrace them for what they are
what they can teach us.
You learn to appreciate the sandbanks
and bask for a while.

You are never alone for long
on the river.
But you will determine as you go along,
with whom you can swim.
And with whom you will sink.
And some of them help you to be
a better swimmer.
A beautiful swimmer.
And the river is wonderful.

Some will make you cry so much that
your tears will fill the river
and become like a torrent.

No one knows what your river
is meant to be.
What it looks like.

When it will end and join the sea.
All you can do is swim
with it
become it
and see what happens.

It will always change
and no matter how hard you kick against it
it will take you with it.
Till it becomes part of something
bigger.

Life is like a river.

LETTING GO

It was Lao Tzu who said:
'When I let go of what I am;
I become what I might be.'

Maybe, we aren't who we think we are.

Can we change the story, the limitations, the type, the restrictions, our opinions, our visions of ourselves?

Is it too late not to see ourselves as simply the end result of genetics, family, experiences, schooling, society, religion, or other people's opinions and beliefs that have been forced on us and though we have questioned them, perhaps even rejected them, the blueprint has remained and shaped us?

Acceptance of ourselves is, it seems, the Holy Grail, achieved after lots of work, growth, wisdom, years, work, work, work on ourselves.

But which self is that? Is it the whole answer? Are we the person we were ten years ago? Or yesterday? Or sixty years ago? Are we dragging behind us a doctrine about ourselves from the past that doesn't actually reflect us now – that doesn't even serve us now?

I think we are capable of being much more than a one-dimensional, accepted version of ourselves.

Maybe we are multi-dimensional beings who constantly change, grow, change, bloom, change, develop, change, change, change.

Maybe, the you that you've come to know and define yourself by, is actually a very outmoded version. It's just that we got stuck somewhere along the way, and like a record player, became stuck on the same repeated song, over and over and over again. We didn't think to stop and change the record. Play a new song.

Have you heard yourself making some of these statements or starting sentences with some of these:

'Oh, I've never been very good at that…'

'No, I'm not like that…'

'Oh, gosh, I could never do that…'

'I've always been like that – that's just who I am.'

'I'm not artistic/creative/sporty/confidant/clever/good with money/good with anything…'

'Yes, I always try to: keep the peace/be a fixer/be sensitive to others' needs first/be a doer/not be lazy.'

'I'm a Virgo/ Capricorn/Aries, that's just me, can't change…'

The list could go on and on and do you see a pattern there? These are all self-limiting beliefs that we have about ourselves.

But why? Do they really reflect who we are now? Do they really reflect who we can be tomorrow?

Are you happy with the beliefs you have about who you are? Or do they hold you back? Do these beliefs keep confirming the type of person you are to yourself and others? Do you really have THAT personality? Or are you so much more?

Have you reached the Holy Grail of self-acceptance and

self-love? Or would you like to change the narrative?

Can we choose to be a different version of ourselves and let the world in on our secret? Did we actually choose the old version or was it thrust upon us?

Maybe, we are not ONLY the person we think we are.

Maybe, there's a lot more to us now and we can blow apart those definitions of ourselves.

If you have ever said that you couldn't sew a button on to save your life, try it.

Maybe you can!

I think that true freedom in life is to realise that we are ever changing, ever expanding, ever beautiful, ever unique individuals. Our personalities can, indeed, change and expand and become whatever we want them to be. You can indeed, teach an old dog, new tricks!

Now, tomorrow, always.

We started out like the little acorn.

Are we still that acorn?

Or have we become the mighty oak?

Change your story.

Change the dialogue.

Update to a truer version.

Believe.

Fly.

Because maybe, just maybe, we aren't who we think we are.

HUMAN

I chased some dreams
That never came true
But I chased them.

I took some chances
That never paid out
But I took them.

I did some things
That I fully regret
But I did them.

I didn't sit and wait
To become someone,
Something
Sometime.
Though sometimes I did.

And I loved
And I lost
And I cried
I hated everything
About my world
And I nearly gave up
But I didn't.

So, what does that make me…
Human.

And I forgave
And accepted
And I left it all
In the past.
And started again.

So where does that leave me now?

Life has no answers
Just questions
And the space between the lines
Is what it gives us
And what we take from it.

I chased a dream
And thought I lost it
But it chased me instead.
And it found me.

So where does that leave me?
It doesn't.

CELEBRATING

You make me laugh.
So funny you are,
yet, wise.
I love your
positive expectations
and your beautiful eyes.
You make me feel adventurous.
So brave you are,
yet, kind.
I love your enquiring nature
And your beautiful mind.
I want to be like you.
So inspiring you are,
yet, humble.
But I cannot be like you.
I stumble…
when I try.
I'm just me,
celebrating the wonder
of who we are.
Unlikely souls
thrown together,
under the same bright star.

THIS IS

To never blame anyone or yourself.

To never hold onto guilt or regret or what's past.

But to understand it.

To embrace the present, however it is.

To never fear the future, but hold on to hope.

To be forgiving of others and yourself.

To accept forgiveness into your heart.

To let go of anger towards others and yourself.

To be open to all views and all opinions.

Even if they differ from your own.

To honour, admire and love the differences.

To have courage to overcome all obstacles.

To embrace every opportunity.

Or make them.

To believe in your people with all their flaws and frailties.

To believe in yourself with your flaws and frailties.

To allow the voyage of ourselves and our story to be true.

And to let it unfold naturally and peacefully.

To go with the flow to see where it leads.

To know that there are miracles everywhere, every day.

Even if we can't see them.

To know that we are a miracle too.

These are the paths we can take.

These are the choices we can make.

This is the power we can own.

This is happiness.

A TRAIL IN THE WOODS

I took a trail of green
and brown
and walked into the woods.
To beautiful sounds
whispering trees.
To cool, fresh air
gentle breezes.
To feeling a part of
all that surrounded me.
Earth, sky, nature.
Freedom.
Coming down to earth.
Coming home to me.
I breathed it all in
to city lungs
starved of clean, pure air.
I followed the path
to the end of the woods.
Through the brown
and the blessed.
Through the goodness
and green.

RATTLED

One crazy evening,
I found myself unexpectedly,
talking to my glass cabinet.
It was rattling at me.
Every time I walked by…
rattle…rattle…rattle.
Walking back again,
rattle…rattle…rattle.

I tried to ignore it but then I realised that,
it doesn't normally rattle…rattle…rattle.
It started to drive me a little crazy.
It was annoying me.
So, I opened the cabinet and asked the glasses
what on earth was wrong here?
Why had they just started to
rattle…rattle…rattle?
No answer.

So, I moved them about a bit.
Swapped a few things around.
Placed them further apart.
Told them to behave and get a life and to stop
rattling.

Then I tested it out;
walked past, back and forth
a couple of times.
Silence.

Later, when I thought about it
I got two things out of that little episode.

One
sometimes, in the midst of
our noisy, hurley-burley,
ridiculous, rattling around
to and fro, life
we all just need a little SPACE!

And

the second thing is…

I might just need

A little rest and space myself…

Cause I've started talking to my cabinet!

(I'm not making this up!!)

Well, and also, maybe you CAN have too many glasses.

MUSIC

One of the most important things in my life has been music. I listen to it, I play it, I write it. I absorb every bit of it into my psyche. It moves me and fills my heart. I cannot be away from it for too long. It is my lifeline, like writing, the two most important things that I do and make me who I am.

I have no particular favourite genre now, though I have had in the past. All types of music have their own beauty. And music I think, is one of the best ways for us to get in touch with our emotions and feelings. It can call to the very core of your soul and your mind. It can give us happy feet and a happy heart or move you so deeply that you feel your life will be changed forever because of it. It will take you far away to distant lands and sometimes, it will bring you home.

That humankind can make this amazing thing called music, is like a miracle to me.

And nature too, can make music if you stop long enough to listen: the sonata of running water, the drum roll of an approaching storm, the wind blowing its trumpet, the endless variety of the birdsong. Even in the silence of night, the earth plays her tune.

As long as the world and the people of this world continue to play and listen to music, I believe that hope will live and beauty will go on.

TILL THE NIGHT IS DONE

Let me sit here in the heart
of this music
and fly for awhile
where you and I can't see.

Let me be in love
with this moment
for ecstasy is nowhere near
as frequent
as it used to be.

Let me stay here for awhile
where dreams live
and love lingers
to become.

Flying high with this music
and these wonderful words
I'm going to sit here
for a lifetime
or till the night
is done
or till the night is done.

Let me be in love with this moment
Let me stay here for awhile
I'm going to sit here in this music
till the night is done
till the night is done.

A GIFT OF LOVE

I hear your notes.
I sing to your music.
I live and breathe
your language.

I am your notes.
I play your music.
I live and breathe
your beauty.

I am the music
and you the notes.
I cannot live or breathe
without your melodies.

The music that comes
into your life
can never be thanked enough
for its timelessness
its gift of laughter, peace
tears, dreams, dance.
Every note,
A gift of love.

SPRING FLOWERS

One of the first lovely signs
that our winter is over,
are the sprinklings everywhere of dandelions
and clover.

On every footpath, backyard
and kids' playing ground
they pop up their flowers
in exultation profound.

They need no tending,
no fertiliser or rain.
They share their delight
without agenda or gain.

The bees are a-buzzing.
Their spring work begun.
And honey will be flowing
now summer has begun.

SPRING FLOWERS

But, in the suburban back shed
there is a threat looming over
the nodding happy heads
of the dandelions and clover.

For out of those sheds
with alarming, noisy power
comes a dragon and beast
in the form of the mower.

City people see the flowers only as enemies
to their God, their almighty green lawn
They are pests! They are weeds!
Off with their heads
they all must be shorn.

The war has begun
for the yellow and white
as the towering beast
decapitates them from sight.

But they are resilient
these tough, happy flowers.
And poke their heads upwards
to laugh at the mowers.

Why do we have this crazy obsession?
Why can't we open our eyes and see
That Nature has given us these beautiful wildflowers
for our delight and for the delight of the bee.

I don't care, I love them and they make me smile.
I look forward to their coming when winter is over.
Here's to the happiness of the sun-kissed dandelions
And the beauty of the soft white sprinklings of clover.

SIMPLE PLEASURES

There's nothing better than soft afternoon rain in Springtime on a quiet Saturday. With a cool breeze shifting between the rain-spotted leaves that has you reaching for a light, warm jacket and a warm cup of something and spying a discarded book. You lay down your work and decide, well, really, it is Saturday after all and it's raining.

    It's one of those Ahh moments.

    Not a lot better than this.

LUCKY

I have been both unlucky and lucky in love in my life. The unlucky times have made me grow. Made me resilient. Made me, eventually, learn to love and rely on myself.

The lucky times have been fewer but memorable.

I got married once. A bit later in life. I decided to take a giant leap of faith and just say, yes.

There were complications for us. It's a story all by itself. But it was, mostly, a fantastic time in my life and I'm so glad I experienced it. The good and the bad. Well, okay, I could have done without the bad!

That relationship was magic in so many ways. And it was a delightful gift when I thought my run had expired.

And it broke my heart.

But, truly, I do believe, that love never dies. It can change shape. It can be buried deep inside. It can be washed away with a dam full of tears. It can be bitter. It can be damaging.

But for me, there was always a connection between us that could not and has not been broken. It was there at the beginning and it is still there. Some indefinable spiritual bond.

I fell in love. I got married. It didn't last. But I was so very lucky to have known love.

THAT'S HOW I KNEW

My heart used to race
every time
you phoned me.
That's how I knew
I loved you.

My heart used to melt
every time
you looked at me.
That's how I knew
you were a miracle.

My heart used to sing
every time
you made me laugh.
That's how I knew
how lucky I was.

My heart used to yearn for you

every time

we were apart.

That's how I knew

you were mine.

And even when we ended

when we knew we couldn't

go on.

My heart was filled with

gratitude.

Because…

You made my heart

race and

melt and

sing and

yearn.

That was the miracle and

it was beautiful.

WHAT COLOUR IS LOVE?

What colour is love?
Brown eyes.
White teeth
in a wide smile.

What does it feel like?
Warm hands
on cold faces
and kisses.

What does love sound like?
Happy laughter.
Sweet whisperings.
The silent sound
of tears.

What place is love?

Here

with you.

Teaching me.

Guiding me.

Unconditionally

accepting me.

What is love?

Love is now.

Hands reaching for each other

and finding.

SOMETIMES

Prayers get answered

Sometimes

Dreams come true

Surprising and confusing

Chasing the doubts

out of you.

Sometimes

Love becomes eternal

Sometimes

Love is all too true

And unrequited love

Sometimes does

come back to you.

Sometimes

I wonder if it's worth it

Sometimes

The tears fall like rain

Just when I think

I can't make it

Hope returns again.

One Beautiful Thing | Carol Davis

Just when the heart

was hurting

And the soul

wrote only sad lines

You came along

to remind me

that maybe

Sometimes

Love can be eternal

Love can be so true

Love can come along

any old time

and surprise you.

Sometimes

It's wrapped in a different way

Sometimes

It's in disguise

I found it

far, far away

In your beautiful, soft, brown

eyes.

MUSIC

Sometimes, I write songs. Sometimes they just write themselves and I have to get up in the middle of the night to take dictation!

This is a quirky little song that wrote itself recently. Sometimes, I don't know what they're all about.

They have their own motivation.

Just like life.

If you analyse it too much, you can lose the whole thread.

This is written for guitar.

A SONG IS A GOOD CONVERSATION
(played slow and mellow)

    C   G

1.Where are you going

    D7   G

my pretty maid?

    Am   G   D7   Am

Over the hills and far away.

    C   G

what does it matter

    D7   G

If I go or stay?

    C   G   Am

The journey is just a beginning.

    C   G

2. Where are you going

    D7   G

my bonny boy?

    Am   G

I'm off to the north

    D7   G

to sing my song.

A SONG IS A GOOD CONVERSATION (played slow and mellow)

   C G

What does it matter

   D7 G

if it's short or long?

   C G Am

A song is a good conversation.

CHORUS

   Am G D7 Am

Over the hills and far away.

   Am G D7 Am

Over the hills and far-aha-away.

   C G

3. Where are you going

   D7 G

my young, sailor friend?

   Am G

I'm going to the moon

   D7 Am

so far away.

C   G
I'm sailing by the stars
D7   G
all night and by day-
C   G   Am
the wind will guide me home.

CHORUS

Am   G   D7   Am
Over the hills and far away.
Am   G   D7   Am
Over the hills and far- aha – away.
C   G
4. Where will I be
D7   G
when I'm old and grey?
Am   G   D7   Am
I'll be the one by the fire's light.
C   G
What does it matter
D7   G
if it's wrong or right?
C   G   Am
It's all been a good conversation.

CHORUS

   Am G D7 Am

Over the hills and far away.

   Am G D7 Am

Over the hills and far- aha- away.

   Am G D7 Am

Off to the hills to run and play.

   C G C

Just want to sing my song…

And this is another song written for the wedding of some friends who found each other across an ocean between two countries.

HOME

Verse 1

There are places you go and you know
you are home.
Every part of you speaks to an energy
Unknown.
Like something called from a long time ago
that beaconed you back
and you had to go.

Chorus

Here I am in this wondrous place.
And here I am in this glorious space.
Yes, I am here in your sweet embrace.
And I am home.
Yes, I'm home.
I am home.

Verse 2

There are people you find
and you take them to your heart.
They become a guiding light
like you've never been apart.
Shining light in the darkness
of your mind.
Your souls are linked and you're
one of a kind.

Chorus

Here I am in this wondrous place.
And here I am in this glorious space.
Yes, I am here in your safe embrace.
And I am home.
Yes, I'm home.
I am home.

Break

Sure, I've been lost

and I've lost my way.

I've given it up and I've

given away.

I've had it taken

and I've had it found.

I've been to the mountain

and the sacred ground…

Chorus

But, here I am in this wondrous place.

And here I am in this glorious space.

Yes, I am here in your soft embrace.

And I am home.

Yes, I'm home.

I am home.

Verse 3

There are places you go and you know
you're far from home.
But the people in your heart
keep you from being all alone.
Then something calls
from far, far away.
And you will go home
for the rest of your days.

Chorus

Here we are in this wondrous place.
And here we are in this glorious space.
Yes, I am here in your sweet embrace.
And I am home.
Yes, I'm home.
We are home.

End

There are places you go
and you know…
You are home.

NATURE

I live in a city. It's been my home for most of my life. This is where my roots are, my beginnings, my family, my friends.

But the call to be immersed in nature is becoming stronger, louder, the older I grow.

I thought that it was just a dream.

Am I running away or running towards?

So many reasons not to.

Shall I just take a LEAP?

I'm full of fear if I do.

I'm full of fear if I don't.

FLY

I need to go back

Back to the mountains and sky

To let my heart fly

ESCAPE

Am I escaping
Up here in my mountain nest
Or have I come home?

I NEED...

To bathe in the sunshine
and let it sink into my bones
and my soul.
To run down a beach with
the sand in my toes
and throw myself into the sea
and let the water heal and
revive me and feel one
with this whole watery planet.
To laugh off this load of
responsibility and worry and
embrace the moment and
think of nothing but happiness.

To walk and walk and walk
till I am one with the earth
and the sky and the breath
of life itself.
To breathe in great lungfuls of fresh,
clean, crisp air.
To flood my body and my brain with the
purity of simply being

I NEED...

in nature.
To grasp life at its most basic
yet learn to let go and dance.
To run wild, care less, love myself more,
Accept, not worry,
fly.

I need…
To throw off the fear shadows,
the burdens and the boundaries
of impending old age.
Throw my heart to the wind
and let it land wherever
it pleases
and plant myself there
like a tree
branching out and up
to life.

I need to be brave and honest and true.
I need
to be.

GONE

I see blue mountains

in the distance

and a road to travel on.

Will I let it go

this time around

or will you find

me gone?

SOUL

I am at peace, trees, earth, sky

Breathing deep within

This is my soul place to be.

FOREST

I have you here in my heart

My forest of love

At peace under your branches.

BRING ME HERE

God of the green earth

beneath my feet

God of the wide-open sky

above me

God of the fields, the hills

and the valleys

God of the far-off

misty mountains

God of the sweet, clean air

that I breathe

God of the bubbling, laughing water

of the brook, the creek and

the river

God of the sounds of the country-

the birds, cows and all manner

of wild things

God of the millions of

stars at night and the

clear moonlight

God of the peace that

surrounds and fills me…

Bring me here.

Bring me here.

Bring me here.

I could weep for the want of it.

LETTING GO

Letting go

All of the anger

Frustration

Disappointments

Guilt

Judgement

Letting go

All of the pain

Just breathing in

Love

Acceptance

Freedom

Wonder

Joy

Belief

Learning

Moving

Dancing

With every moment

Singing

My own sweet tune

Embracing

All that is

Breathing in the love

Breathing out the love

Letting go

Amen.

BETTER

for Elaine

I'm going to sit on the beach
Till the sun goes down
I'm going to sit on the beach forever.
I'm going to sit on the beach
As long as it takes…
To feel better.

And then you came along.

And we sat on the beach
Till the sun went down.
We sat on the beach together.
We sat on the beach
As long as it took.
And we felt much better.

WOULDN'T I?

If I had travelled less, worked more, been smart and vigilant; I would be a lot more secure right now.

Wouldn't I?

If I'd taken my head out of the clouds, been more sensible and kept my feet on the ground, I'd have a lot less regrets now.

Wouldn't I?

I wrote the next poem nearly forty years ago.
I managed to get to a couple of these places.

CALLING TO ME

India, China
The seas of Japan
Calling to me, just
As hard as they can.

India, China
Tokyo Rose
How do I get there
Nobody knows.

India, China
Ancient Tibet
I'm taking the long road
But I'll get there yet.

CALLING TO ME

India, China
Vast Himalay
Tomorrow is just
A step from today.

Old llama, good sooth
Ye aesthetic, wise sage
Make me a part
Of your history page.

Take me and mould me
And set my soul free
In China, India and the Japanese sea.

SUMMER AND WINTER

I am watching the dying rays
of a sunset, sinking into the last
days of summer.
And the mists of the spirit of the mountains
are flying freely
and silently.

I am in awe.

And half of me is here
flying away with them
And half of me is with you
and the mountains
and valleys
of another world
in the last days
of winter.

FOR CHRIS

In distant fields
I spoke your name.
Your voice rose high
on the wind-horse flags.
Your smile sparkled
in the sun-lit snow.
And you walked in happiness
eternal.

A thousand feet high
have I climbed for you.
To fulfil a wish
expressed long before
the knowing of the
ending.

You would have loved
this eyrie temple.
Looking down on your
spirit world
your heart-home.

Flames and smoke
prayers and song
rise to the occasion.
And to the blue-
so blue.

I see you here
walking these trails.
Sitting on a rock
smiling.

My friend
I will miss you all the days
of my life.
Yet you will be closer
than a tear to me.
Watching over
looking out
waiting for reunion.
How blessed we were.

In distant fields
I speak your name.
Remembering.

YOU AND I

You and I
we've walked the
wild places.
Gone searching for adventure
and other possibilities.
We've muddied our lives
in far-flung cesspools;
become millionaires on
memories and stories.
And we've loved and laughed
mostly at our own
foolish endeavours.

What's the tally at the end
do you suppose?
Will we have rated up there
with the best?
Perhaps they'll say we should have
invested, settled down,
watched documentaries,
saved for a home
superannuated.

Ahh, but Chris,
we saw Everest by moonlight
and climbed for a closer view,
a different view,
another perspective.
Through tears and sweat
and shattered nerves,
we soldiered on
and begged for more.

You and I, we walked the wild places.
Daring to dream
of freedom and
and something …more.
And the cost is never counted.
And the journey never ends.

I wrote these last two poems for my dear friend, Chris.
I had wanted, needed to go to Nepal and the Himalayas for a long time but kept putting it off.

And then my sister Anne introduced me to Chris and her husband who had been there and were going again. I was convinced to go with them.

Chris became my guiding light and my best friend and started in me another beautiful story that encompassed years of trekking and loving that part of the world and its people.

I took her there again one last time when she was sick and facing the greatest fear that we can face in life. I was reluctant to do so but she insisted.

Her courage, her strength, her humility and her passion amazed me and everyone with whom she came into contact, on that last walk.

It's many years since she left us to walk that ultimate trek that we will all make one day. But I have never forgotten her and will always love her and her beautiful heart.

The journey never ends. Xxx

WE ARE ONE

I am an eagle soaring
Over the hills and the plains
I am the son of the sun calling
Calling out your names.

I am the spirit of a breeze blowing
Down to the valley of dreams
I am all of your hopes flowing
Into life's rivers and streams.

Don't falter, don't follow
Don't wait for a sign
I am here, I am there
I am gone.
I'll challenge your every
Belief and feeling
I'll fly you away from your home.

I am the sound of music playing
The spirit, siren call
I am the irresistible urge failing
To win the race or fall.

I am a single candle burning
One bright, eternal flame
Bright as the son of the sun shining
And calling out your name.

Don't falter, don't follow
Don't leave it too late
I am lost, I am alone
I am you
I'll take you to heaven
By myth or by fate
I am the all too true.

You are the brightness of the eyes glowing
The eyes of the son of the sun
You are the completeness of every soul
Growing
You are me
I am you
We are one.

THE TIME OF YOUR LIFE

One foot after the other, walking

Up the steep hill, puffing

Through the dappled shade, slightly shivering

Along the brook, babbling

Through my favourite stand of trees, wavering in the breeze

Down the valley, smiling

In a field of flowers, laughing

at how good it is to walk this earth

from the time of childhood

to now.

When I was a child and asleep

I would have a recurring dream of walking, walking

Till I walked far out of this city

This city that I still live and walk in.

I didn't know where I was going

And I still don't.

I have walked far away in other places, many years

many travels.

I have learned that…

It is not in the dreams you dream

But in the life you never dreamed of

It is not in the paths you take

But the steps you make along the way

It is not about the journey's end or the time it took you to get there

But it is about the journey itself

And the time of your life

In a field of flowers, laughing

Down the valley, smiling

Through my favourite stand of trees, wavering in the breeze

Along the brook, babbling

Through the dappled shade, slightly shivering

Up the steep hill, puffing

One foot at a time,

still walking.

REQUIEM

Wrap me up in a soft, warm blanket.
Put wildflowers in my hair.
Then release me quietly and lovingly
into the wild mountain air.

For this is my life's everlasting.
This is my journey's end.
This is all my heart's yearnings
Here where my soul will mend.

And I will run in the wild mountain grasses.
I'll float in the cold, running streams.
I'll fly with the currawongs and eagles.
I'll sing the songs of my dreams.

Wrap me up in a soft warm blanket.
Place wildflowers in my hair.
Let me run with the wild mountain grasses.
Let me float on the sweet, clean air.
For this is life everlasting.
This is the best of the best.
This is my soul's beginning.
This is my journey's rest.

LIGHT

Like so many people (or should that say, all of us?), I too, have struggled with my mental health over the years. I have waged a battle with the black dog of depression, anxiety, PTSD, etc. When I was younger, I blamed myself. I thought that there was something wrong with me, not being able to control it. Or I blamed circumstances, such as not being happy or not achieving want I wanted. Being in the wrong place. And then the between times, when the dark cloud lifted and I achieved some clarity, I felt guilty for the way I had felt. I felt responsible. I felt less than...

Little by little, I learned about the condition of depression and came to understand it in a new, more accepting light. I got to know my triggers and to take notice of them. I accepted the help I needed to live with it, to give it a name and to honour myself because of and in spite of it.

The thing is that sometimes, it can be very difficult to see a beautiful thing. Even if it's just one beautiful thing. There are days when beautiful just does not come into your vocabulary. You feel lost, disempowered, hopeless, desperate and alone.

The following few poems are for those days. The days when you can't even see the light at the end of the tunnel. Because it seems to be just one long, dark tunnel. I've been there. I know it. I know that darkness.

But believe me, there is always a light. There is always a beautiful thing. It may be a long way, away — so far away, you just can't see it. That is why they say:

It is not when you see it, that you believe.

It is when you believe it, that you will see.

But it is there.

And it may come in a totally different way than you thought it would.

Sometimes, to have hope is the beautiful thing.

Sometimes, it is faith.

But always and forever, it is the beauty that you find in your own heart that will help you understand and accept and finally and ever so brilliantly, to see.

IDENTITY

Do you know me?

Do I know myself?

Or did you just decide to label me

Anyway?

Whatever.

Doesn't matter.

I shall just shuffle

back to my shelf.

Safe.

Alone, but safe.

Scared, but safe.

Put me in a box

and tuck me away

from prying hands

and careless thoughts

and me

I shall be quite

quiet here.

Alone, but quiet.

Scared, but quiet.

IDENTITY

Do you know me?
I have forgotten
who I am.
Was.
Where am I going?
What dreams did I have?
Was I part
of someone else's
plans?
Did I belong
somewhere?
Put me back
behind the wall
where I won't fall.
I'll be alone, but not fallen.
Scared, but not broken.
Is this heaven
or hell?
Death
or dying?

Do you know me?

The question seems familiar.

Perhaps I asked someone before

a long time ago

before I was

labelled.

Shelved.

Boxed.

Walled.

Perhaps I shall just fall

anyway.

And make a splash

and feel my way

back

carefully

quietly

to my identity.

ONE LITTLE BOAT

One little boat,
sitting in the harbour.
One little boat,
setting out to sea.

One little boat,
tethered to a mooring.
One little boat
not free.

Am I stuck safely
in the harbour?
Or have I let go enough
to set sail upon the sea?

One little thought,
can change the course
of a lifetime.
One small step,
can set me free.

One little boat,
in the shallows
not moving.
One little boat,
with the wind
in its sails.

One little boat,
never achieving.
One little boat,
not afraid to fail.

All of the little boats,
have their own story.
All of the little boats,
make their own
history.

I am one little boat,
waiting in the harbour.
One little boat
is me
looking out to sea.

WILL I?

I watch a wilting flower
petals drooping,
then dropping off.

I feel like that flower.
I have drooped,
and dropped.

Watching that flower
makes me feel like
weeping.
And sleeping
under the covers.
And never coming out.

I don't want to be
a wilting flower forever.
I want to hold my head up
under the sun.
And come out smiling.

Will I?
Will I smile again?
And believe?

Today, I bought a single,
Beautiful pot, with one
growing sunflower.
To remind me
of what it feels like
to live.

One Beautiful Thing | Carol Davis

NEVER FORGET

Some days are just plain horrible.
They're like the evil fairy just mucked everything up
before you even got out of bed.
Hard to see the beautiful thing
on those days.

No beautiful smile
or surprising laughter.
No gorgeous vista
or walk in the wild.
No warm conversation
with a complete stranger or with anyone.
Even the sunset is grey.

And everything is wrong, wrong, wrong.
What stupid red leaf on a sea of green?

But there is always one thing,
even if you don't believe it.
There is always one constant,
even if you can't see it.
The most beautiful thing of all.
The one thing that counts the most.

Better than a sunset or
a beautiful smile.
Better than any walk in the woods
could ever be.
Better than the ocean at sunrise.
Better than all the stars
in the night sky.
Better than a thousand red leaves
on a sea of green.

It is there in the beginning.
It will be there in the end.
Evil fairy or not.
Every day.
The gift.

It is you.

And it is me.

All of us.

Made beautiful.

Open your eyes
and your heart
and your mind.

Never forget.

FINDING HOME

I suspect you hide
much more than you show.

I feel you stay
when you want to go.

I think your poor heart
is broken in two.

I suspect you have lost
the way to you.

All is well.
Take your time.
Nothing else matters
but the now you own.

All is well.
Take your time.
Leave all the other stuff behind.
And find your way back home.

IF

If happiness
was a drop of water…
my heart would be
an ocean.

If love
was a single flame…
my heart would set
the world on fire.

If peace
was one tiny star…
then you would have helped
my heart to be…
an entire galaxy.

STILL LOOKING

So, that's me.
Or some of me anyway.
For we are all complex beings
Just trying to find our way.
Maybe we can change ourselves
or not.
Maybe we can change our world
or not.
But I do believe…
The beauty is in the trying.
The answer is in the striving.
Life is such a crazy journey, don't you think?
May as well enjoy ourselves a little along the way.
Cry some tears.
Laugh.
Show up.

I'm still looking out for it

Every day.

Some days, it's hard to find.

And sometimes

It's simple.

A red leaf

On a sea of green…

One.

Beautiful.

Thing.

Keep looking.

Carol. 2024

www.ingramcontent.com/pod-product-compliance
Lightning Source LLC
Chambersburg PA
CBHW041218070526
44584CB00001B/5